I0421637

Why Are They Like That? Gay Men

Questions you've dared to ask, answered by real people, celebrities and experts

A book series based on the award-winning sharing project that's captured worldwide attention helping people in their personal, social and business relationships

Phillip J. Milano

For Robin, Jacob, Lucas and Ben

Publisher:
Y Forum
yforum@yforum.com

ISBN: 978-1-07-950340-1

Cover and interior layout by Sandy Weber,
Key 3 Creative, Jacksonville, Florida
Cover photo credit: Rawpixel. Stock photo for illustrative purposes
only; any person depicted is a posed model.

Content based in part on the popular Y? sharing project and Dare
to Ask column

Find out more about the author, upcoming books and speeches at
www.phillipmilano.com, www.facebook.com/PhillipJMilano or
@PhillipMilano.

Books In This Series

Why Are They Like That? Blacks

Why Are They Like That? Whites

Why Are They Like That? Hispanics

Why Are They Like That? Asians

Why Are They Like That? Gay Men

Why Are They Like That? Lesbians

Why Are They Like That? Women

Why Are They Like That? Men

Why Are They Like That? Rich and Poor

Why Are They Like That? Religious (or not)

Why Are They Like That? Disabled People

Why Are They Like That? Young and Old

Praise for the Y? sharing project and the book "I Can't Believe You Asked That!" (Perigee)

"Milano is quietly revolutionizing cross-cultural communication..."
- Pulitzer Prize-winning columnist Leonard Pitts

"If you've ever hesitated to ask a question because you think it might be considered insensitive or impolitic, now is your chance ... Nothing is considered out of bounds..."
- CNN Headline News

"(It) tells more about who we are and how we feel about each other than you're likely to learn from a dozen sociology texts…"
- Washington Post News Service

"Mr. Milano has dared to open the field of debate to the maximum…"
- Le Monde, Paris

"(A) remarkable contribution to cross-cultural understanding…"
- The (London) Guardian

"A truly rare achievement … has the potential to have a profound impact on the way we all see and understand each other..."
- Playboy magazine

"It's an incredible book. It diffuses everything ... Nothing is off limits, and the questions have that childlike honesty to them..."
- Dee Snider, Twisted Sister; host, "Dee Snider Radio"

"A take-no-prisoners attitude prevails between the volume's covers . . . This book is hard to put down..."
- Midwest Book Review

"A+ (highest rating) … Everything you wanted to know but were afraid to ask gets tackled here ..."
- Entertainment Weekly

4

CONTENTS

Introduction 6

Do gay men not typically 'date up'? 8

Muscling in on a man's bicep, tricep, inguinal crease... 10

Is it OK for girls to dig guys who don't dig girls? 12

Do straight men still freak about having a gay male friend? 14

How can you be gay and crack open a Bible? 16

Is gaydar an acquired skill, or a natural talent? 18

The first time, ever I saw … my gay body 20

You can look, and you can touch her, if you're gay 22

Sensitive, caring, 5 years old … and gay? 24

Listen up: being deaf doesn't bring on the gay-ness 26

Does campy behavior cramp other gays' style? 28

I now pronounce you husband and husband? 30

The O.U.T.L.O.U.D. Method to Dialogue 32

About the Author 34

Speeches and Appearances 35

Introduction

Why Are They Like That? is a series of books based on an award-winning worldwide sharing project in which real people, experts and celebrities talk about things that make us different from each other. Silly things. Sad things. Funny things. Profound things.

Read with an open mind and we believe that by the time you're finished you'll have a much better understanding of how to make more and real friends, money and love. It's that simple.

Why? Because this isn't about trying to get ahead with diversity training. We are well beyond that. According to the Census Bureau, by 2050 the United States will have no racial or ethnic minority.

No, this is about moving past talking about how to understand each other to talking to each other. Right now.

That's why there's no agenda to these books other than getting the conversation going. We can discuss studies and methods for elevating social consciousness all we want, but there is no substitute for real dialogue.

That's where Why Are They Like That? stands apart from other books on the topic. You will see how people talk about their real differences of race, religion, sex, disability and more.

The success of the approach is proven: It's based on the ground-breaking Y? website project, blog and column that have attracted millions of visitors and worldwide media attention.

Our hope is that by reading, you will become more comfortable asking and answering the questions yourself, expecting the unexpected in return and helping change the ground rules for how we learn from and about each other. To that end, we wrap up each book in the series with our O.U.T.L.O.U.D. Method for Dialogue, with tips to help you get your own conversations started. Ultimately, that is what this effort is all about.

After all, if you want to make more friends, money and love, you better know the people you're talking to, selling to or opening to. Knowledge isn't just power. It's all power.

Enjoy.

Phillip J. Milano
Founder, Y?

Do gay men not typically 'date up'?

They asked:

I'm called handsome by some, but I think I am unattractive. I recently started accepting my sexuality and realized I am gay. Is there acceptance in the gay community for "ugly" people?

N.N., 17, male, Minnesota

You said:

Young metros who go to clubs might desire a particular look, but that is not ubiquitous to all gay men. Most of my gay friends are just average-looking. They say there's someone for everyone. Just try not to obsess over your appearance. That kind of vain insecurity is unappealing to all stripes of sexual orientation.

Dot, female, Los Angeles

Different people find different features attractive, so I'd suggest believing the people who call you handsome. While there are certain features that turn me off (mustaches), in general, chemistry is more important to me than looks.

Charles, 56, gay, Oakland, Calif.

We found:

Let's not forget, gay males aren't just gay, they're male, too. That means that, just like many straight guys, many gay guys are really big on looks first, says gay dating expert and Huffington Post columnist Mike Alvear (Gaydatingsuccess.net), author of books including "Men Are Pigs But We Love Bacon."

"There's definitely a standard by which everyone is compared, and it is typically young, tall, muscular and hopefully with a big package. It's our version of big [breasts]," said Alvear, who co-hosted HBO's "The Sex Inspectors" and writes books on how to attract hot gay guys.

What makes the whole hunkiness thing so suffocating for many gay men is that there's no opposite sex — i.e., women — to blunt the sharp focus on looks, he said.

"Women don't put as much emphasis on male appearance. So you can walk down the street and see a gorgeous woman with a fat, ugly toad of a straight guy, but in gay life you'll almost never see a fat-ugly-toad guy with a beautiful guy, unless he's an escort."

That means gay men can't usually date "out of their league," whereas a straight guy can often find a partner to judge him first on things other than appearance, like personality, experience, humor or wealth, Alvear said.

"Gay men aren't shallow, but like straight men, they have priorities. Research shows it's an evolutionary principle with men in general."

A Harvard University study on facial attraction, for example, found that gay and straight men both like faces more synonymous to the sex they're attracted to. Specifically, gay guys are really into masculine-faced men (broad jaw and forehead, etc.) while straight guys prefer feminine-faced women (tapered chin, big lips, narrow forehead).

Meanwhile, prior research also found women prefer more masculine male faces when ovulating, possibly for procreation reasons.

"You are biologically inclined to look for markers of fertility in the sex to which you are attracted. It's in the genes," Alvear said.

Muscling in on a man's bicep, tricep, inguinal crease…

They asked:

Straight women and gay men: What is the most attractive muscle on a man?

David B., Los Angeles

You said:

His brain.

Lady J., 24, Los Angeles

Abs are the most attractive. My second choice would be their chest, as long as they aren't overly built ("man-boobs").

Gregory, 17, gay, Minn.

I find the thighs very attractive, but only if they are covered in thick body hair. I also like 'em to have a bit of a paunch.

Trisha, 27, Flint, Mich.

Stomach (often indicates a low body fat percentage) and legs/butt (very functional muscles).

Jason, 29, gay, New York

We found:

Aww. His brain. And a paunch. Neil deGrasse Tyson and Zach Galifianakis, sleep well.

For the rest of us, here's the wake-up call: A Men's Health magazine poll found that women's Top 10 male muscle preferences were, in descending order: strong hamstrings, large biceps, big chest, money line (the inguinal crease between the torso and inner thigh), rock-hard calves, sculpted shoulders, broad back, nice butt, powerful forearms and six-pack abs. AskMen.com's own list, descending order: Sharply shaped shoulders, Chiseled chest,

Bulging biceps, Luscious lips, Tantalizing tongue, Hygienic hands, Honed hips, Awesome abs, Primped penis, Buff butt.

For gay guys, proportion seems a bigger deal. One study published in the International Journal of Men's Health reported gay men like lower waist-to-chest ratios on other men. A V-shape may indicate a powerful upper body.

Some studies suggest rising male "muscle dysmorphia": they gaze in the mirror and see "puny and frail."

In "The Adonis Complex: The Secret Crisis of Male Body Obsession," researchers say college men in one study felt women preferred a male body with 30 pounds more muscle than they currently had. But an accompanying study found women actually desired just an "ordinary male body without added muscle."

Roberto Olivardia, clinical psychologist at Harvard Medical School and co-author of "The Adonis Complex," told us:

Women like diversity. "A healthy body, nice skin, a nice smile … Some muscle and a strong upper body."

Gay men desire in other men what they idealize in themselves. "A strong jaw line, full head of hair, taller height, large penis, fit, muscular body, strong upper body. … It is more about the visual. This has nothing to do with being gay … (and) everything to do with being male."

Survival is at play. "Studies show that during ovulation, women are more attracted to traditionally strong, masculine-looking men. … Interestingly, when not in ovulation, women tend to prefer less traditionally masculine-looking men. They are more attracted to men who they feel are more emotionally committed."

Women are getting more demanding. "Media imagery has just recently been focusing on the male body as a commodity, and both sexes have responded to that."

Is it **OK** for girls to dig guys who don't dig girls?

They asked:

I'm attracted to gay men. My boyfriend has a problem with this. What is wrong with me?

Gina, 21, Dallas

You said:

Sunshine, nothing is wrong with you. Gay males are a Safety Zone!

Paul, gay, Akron, Ohio

Of course he has a problem with that! You're attracted to men with qualities he apparently doesn't have. That said, most women wouldn't blame you. There is a reason for the cliché "All the great men are either married or gay." Gay men tend to take better care of themselves and be more stylish. They tend to be less macho and sexist in how they relate to women.

Lynne, Arlington, Va.

I have plenty of female friends. It's because if they ever catch me looking at their chest, they know I'm trying to read their T-shirt rather than get my jollies.

Brian, 18, gay, Minnesota

Why is this a problem for your boyfriend? Is he homophobic? Or maybe he's unsure how "gay" some of these guys really are.

Rich, 46, gay, Seattle

It boils down to insecurity and ignorance.

Paul, 27, Austin, Texas

These friendships have the advantage of being platonic, which attracts many women because of the "forbidden fruit" mentality — you want exactly what you can't have. But if the issue is sensitivity and empathy, many straight and bisexual men are just as caring.

Chris, 24, bisexual female, Chicago

Would your boyfriend think it was weird if he found a hot lesbian attractive? Hot is hot, regardless of sexual orientation.

Jean, 39, lesbian, California

We found:

Straight gal/gay guy? That's touching — with no touching!

Some straight women enjoy the lack of sexual tension when with gay men, said writer and filmmaker Tom Dolby (tomdolby.com), co-editor of the book "Girls Who Like Boys Who Like Boys."

"There's no issue in terms of who's going home with whom," he said.

Clichés about straight women and their gay pals swooning over shopping and dishing about men are superficial, though, noted Dolby, who wrote and co-directed the film "Last Weekend" starring Patricia Clarkson.

"I think most straight female/gay male friendships have at their heart a real sense of mutual understanding that may be lacking from other friendships and relationships."

While he didn't think Gina was off-base to hang with gay men, she should consider what her penchant means, he suggested.

"If it's to the exclusion of all other friendships and relationships, then I'd say there's something wrong. ... I think single girls can sometimes use gay men as a crutch when they are not in relationships," he said. "She might want to ask herself what she's getting from her gay male friendships that she's not getting from her boyfriend."

And hopefully she isn't the kind angling to "turn" a gay man.

"I think that's a pretty futile endeavor!" Dolby said.

Do straight men still freak about having a gay male friend?

They asked:

Why do straight men think they can be "just friends" with a woman but can't with a gay man?

Duane, gay, black, Washington, D.C.

You said:

They don't want to be labeled gay. My boyfriend makes faces or groans when I talk about gay marriage and equal rights. He admits he has no problem with gay people but is so accustomed to living up to the standards that men can only be manly that he automatically makes expressions even though he doesn't mean to.

Shaina, Fort Worth

Men are thought to lack sexual self-control. Homosexuality is considered abnormal, and to too many people is evidence of even less self-control. You'll notice how homosexuality is too often equated with pedophilia, because if you would do something as crazy as have sex with men you're probably crazy enough to have sex with a child — and in the end crazy enough to pursue a heterosexual man even though he's not interested.

Omelio, 28, Philadelphia

The majority of people don't believe homosexuality is abnormal, and most know it has nothing to do with pedophilia. Psychologists point to insecurities about one's own sexuality as the reason some people are uncomfortable around gays.

D., Los Angeles

We found:

All straight guys have had close gay male friends. Sure, you were in third grade together and neither of you knew it, but own it now. In a pinch you can use it to sound cultivated.

As adults, though, too many hetero men are still uncomfortable getting friendly — er, bonding — with a gay dude, said Jim Sullivan (boyfriend101.com), a relationship coach and author of "Boyfriend 101: A Gay Guy's Guide to Dating, Romance and Finding True Love."

"Imagine ... what it's like for a straight man to deal with the possibility he might be perceived as less of a man if he's hanging out with a gay man, or that he might be [perceived as] gay?"

Sullivan said straight men under 30 tend to get less bent out of shape over befriending someone gay. And any man who's around a gay guy long enough often can be softened up. In his therapy work that has involved intensive weekend group sessions, often straight men come away open to friendship, reaching a point where they see that "Jim Sullivan is just a guy who wants love, has affections, fears."

His advice to wary straight men is to just go with the flow — and not be nervous about a "come-on."

"If there ever was some inappropriate action or flirting, just say 'I'm not interested, I just want to be friends.' ... Don't broach the topic unless he makes an overture. Otherwise, if you say, 'Well I want to be friends but I think you'll come on to me' ... what arrogance!"

And gay guys: Don't focus on your "gayness" all the time, he said. Think about what you may have in common with a straight man — whether it's politics, choice of music or, in Sullivan's case, a passion for basketball and Irish culture.

How can you be gay and crack open a Bible?

They asked:

A lot of people say they are gay and Christian. Isn't the Bible against homosexuality?

Natalie, 18, straight, Australia

You said:

Homosexuality is never explicitly outlawed in the Bible. But the position of the Bible is homophobic. A punishment is attached to the sexual act, namely stoning.

Michael, 21, New York

The Bible is the living word of God — how much more "law" do you need? I love smoking pot, so I justified it because it didn't actually say in the Bible not to. But we know it is against the law. ... Don't try and justify something you know you are not supposed to do.

Joshua, 28, straight, Oregon

Leviticus condemns the act of homosexual sex, not homosexuality per se. ... In the New Testament, Paul condemns things Jesus never seemed to worry about.

Elizabeth, 18, straight, Mansfield, Ohio

The Old Testament condemns usury and wearing clothing woven of two different fibers. Yet Christianity has moved beyond enforcing these. So get thee behind me, Satan, in thy gabardine and polyester weave slacks.

Ben, 31, gay, Sydney, Australia

Corinthians 6:9 warns: "Do you not know the unrighteous will not inherit the kingdom of God? ... neither the immoral, nor idolaters, nor adulterers, nor homosexuals ... will inherit God's kingdom." We all do well to heed this warning.

Holly, 28, Annapolis, Md.

Most gay-baiting Christians who come to save us lost sheep can't withstand more than five minutes of detailed Bible reading before they give up and look for someone more vulnerable.

Mark, 39, gay, Dallas

We found:

Depending on your Bible, Corinthians 6:9-10 refers to homosexuals ... or not. Some versions instead say "abusers of themselves with mankind," and some scholars say Paul would've used a common Greek term at the time — paiderasste — if he wanted to refer to sex between males.

Biblical bickering aside, Justin Lee, founder of the 14,000-member Gay Christian Network (gaychristian.net), said many people talk of "Side A" or "Side B" gay Christians.

Side A'ers support gay marriage and same-sex relations; Side B'ers don't and remain celibate.

Side B gay Christians say " 'I agree the Bible condemns gay sex, so I don't have it,' " said Lee, author of "Torn: Rescuing the Gospel from the Gays-vs.-Christians Debate," who grew up Southern Baptist and now falls into the Side A camp.

Many Christians maintain gay people can't change their orientation — they condemn the behavior alone, he said.

Side A proponents say that doesn't go far enough, and that the Bible's stance isn't about "loving, monogamous gay relationships," but sexual behavior in the context of idolatry or pederasty.

"As Christians ... we disagree, but we love one another in the midst of disagreement," Lee said. "I believe the Bible is not anti-gay, but many people use it that way. And I'm not willing to concede it to them."

Is gaydar an acquired skill, or a natural talent?

They asked:

Do gay people who have gaydar have it from birth, or do they learn it?

Roland, 16, straight, Fleming Island

You said:

My gaydar's always been inherent, but I didn't realize it for what it was until I was well into my teens. I've always been drawn to people who were gay (or who later turned out to be gay), but it's only since I started actively thinking about it that I realized this. Gaydar uses a lot of different cues, including voice, language, dress, movement, reaction to people and many more things, but I very rarely actually have to think about all these things and put them together to work out if someone's gay or not.

Pic A., 20, pansexual, United Kingdom

I think we all have certain abilities that, if we don't use them, we lose. This extends to things like psychics and artists, etc. That said, I think "gaydar" is one of those natural talents that some people find easier to use than others. However, I don't know if most people know what "gaydar" is. I know I certainly didn't recognize what it was when I was growing up.

S. Rollison, 49, bisexual female, Pennsylvania

We found:

Let's get right to the most important question raised here: No, Pic isn't attracted to stovetop cooking devices or people who can fly and never grow up. Let's just say, in our little way, that a pansexual is open to all the possibilities.

Gaydar itself, the alleged ability to tell whether people who watch "UFC Fight Night," "The American Outdoorsman" or "Project Runway" are gay, is harder to pin down.

There's no legit research that establishes the biological reality of gaydar, said Erik Libey, a gay educator and associate director of LGBT & Rural Services at AIDS Care in Rochester, N.Y.

"It's not like we're producing pheromones that other gays can pick up on," he said. "Even some gay people will say they have finely tuned gaydar, while others say no, they're always flirting with people who are hopelessly straight."

The problem with "gaydar" is that it can become rooted in stereotypes, many bigoted, about straight or gay people.

"There are effeminate heterosexual men who love San Francisco, and there are masculine gay men who would rather spend a week camping in Colorado than a day in the Castro in San Francisco," Libey said.

But c'mon, how do you tell?

Context and syntax, for starters, he said.

"For instance, someone using the word 'partner,' it's not typical of straight people to use that ... so that would cause your ears to perk up," he said. "Or, you meet someone for the first time, and they talk about their fabulous vacation to Fire Island [N.Y.], that might be a marker."

Overall, caution is the rule.

"Even as a very open gay man, the only way for me to know for sure is to ask, and rely on their information. That said, my need to know one's orientation is not very high. If you want to take someone home, yes, you need to know, but your cashier or waiter?"

The first time, ever I saw … my gay body

They asked:

Do gay people enjoy looking at their own bodies in the mirror?
Tom W., 68, straight, Miami

You said:

No! I have never been turned on by seeing myself in the buff.
J.P., 35, lesbian, Fort Lauderdale

I think it's like tickling yourself: It doesn't work.

J.K., Chicago

I don't think the average homosexual would get any more excited by that image than, say, Tom Cruise would. Tom W. may be confusing homosexuality with narcissism.

Robert, Jacksonville

It's not common, but not unheard of, either. In 25 years of being out, I have run across a number of bodybuilders who definitely were turned on by the man in the mirror. I've even met a couple of guys who never took their eyes off themselves!
Mark, 49, gay, New York

Quite a few gay men are more interested in the maintenance and appearance of themselves, not because of self-attraction but because we know what type of looks we are interested in and try to become our ideal person. That rings true for me. If I find myself attractive, I tend to be more confident around other people who are attractive.

Ben S., 29, gay, *Lima*, Ohio

Ha. To be honest, no. But then again, I don't sit there and just pose, either. I mean, don't get me wrong, from what I hear I'm pretty attractive, but no.

Andy, 21, gay, Alabama

Yes. I like my body.

Jay, 36, gay, Chicago

I sometimes think, "you still look good" when I get out of the shower, but that's not attraction, just a (realistic?) appraisal.

Tom, 57, gay, Chicago

We found:

We reflected (but did not primp or preen) and then called Eric Marcus, author of such books as "Is It A Choice?," "Making Gay History" and the No. 1 New York Times-bestselling "Breaking the Surface," an autobiography of Olympic diving great Greg Louganis,

"You bet some of us look, but so do straight guys. They check out their own six-packs and legs, too," he said.

As far as a gay guy enjoying what he sees in the mirror, it depends on what he looks like — and what he's looking for, Marcus said.

"If a gay man has a spectacular physique, and it's the kind of body he's attracted to, I'd think it's quite exciting to see that. But I would also think you'd dissociate yourself from the person in the mirror; instead you'd objectify the body in the mirror so it's a male body and not yours, so you get the biggest bang for the buck . . . unless you're really into yourself."

Much of what he's seen is at the gym, where guys are working out and trying to make themselves look better.

"What's better than having five to 10 mirrors around so you can see your body in five different ways?" he said with a laugh.

Overall, though, a lot of straight people linger in the looking glass, too, Marcus said.

"Everybody knows someone who's into themselves."

You can look, and you can touch her, if you're gay

They asked:

Why don't many women seem to mind being touched by a gay man in ways that would get a straight man slapped?

Steve, 42, Chattanooga, Tenn.

You said:

Cuz, hello, it's a gay dude.

Marisa, 15, Illinois

We are not doing it out of lust.

Tim, gay, West Palm Beach

Women want to feel attractive, and attention from a gay man helps that — with the added bonus of not wondering what the guy's motives are.

JJ, 30, lesbian, San Diego

I was at a party and saw a man blatantly fondling a woman! She said, "It's OK for a gay man." Why is it OK "because he doesn't enjoy it"? No wonder women can't find a man.

Nick F., Seattle

I think deep down inside every gay man is really straight. They are fascinated by us girls!

Tiff, 22, Alta Loma, Calif.

It's because the gay men are giving something rather than taking something.

Lynne, Arlington, Va.

If you're jealous of gay men being able to grope women, just pretend you're gay and you can get all the action you want! (That's a joke, by the way.)

Susan, 21, Novi, Mich.

It feels comfortable, safe. And there's a little "Hmmm, does he or does he not find me attractive?" And if he does — wow, how attractive must I be to get a gay man wanting to touch me?

Beth, 25, Greenville, S.C.

We found:

Right, we get it: The "gay men aren't threatening" idea.

As the patient man behind the busy New York sandwich counter might say: "What else?"

For one, straight women do like being around male energy, and it's nice to not have to say "I just want to be friends," says gay advice columnist Mike Alvear (www.Gaydatingsuccess.net), former co-host of HBO's Sex Inspectors late-night series.

"I've seen gay guys do what would be considered sexually molesting (a straight woman), but why do straight guys wrestle around on a football field or slap each other's butts? It's a way of expressing affection."

Still, there are limits, he says. "If I as a gay male put my hand where it shouldn't be, I'd get slapped, too."

Often, straight women hit on gay guys. Usually they aren't aware the man is gay, but sometimes are and take a shot anyway, Alvear said.

"I've heard 'You haven't been with the right woman -- I'm her.' Just change the subject or say, 'I'm more interested in that guy there.'"

A last note: People may also not realize that lots of straight women are in love with their gay male friends, he said. "So if anything, women would probably want their gay friend to touch them."

Sensitive, caring, 5 years old ... and gay?

They asked:

My 5-year-old son is very sensitive and fastidious. Last night, he told me he was going to marry his friend, a boy. I will love him the same no matter what, but it does worry me and scares his dad to death. When do boys begin to know something is different about them?

Renee, 35, San Antonio

You said:

I always knew I was "different" but didn't associate this with sexuality until 11 or 12. Others know at a very young age, around 5 to 7. Your boy may know he likes boys, so make sure your husband tries not to scold him for acting "gay," as this could be taken as rejection.

Kevin, 17, Los Angeles

It's more likely he's just developing his personality, and his fastidiousness may be a blessing in disguise. At least you won't have to nag him to keep his room clean.

M.C., 31, male, Omaha, Neb.

I know a lot of very camp straight men! Equally, young tomboy girls who climb trees are not necessarily lesbians in the making.

David, 45, United Kingdom

We found:

This boy needs a stronger male role model pronto, says the Rev. Jim Venice, founder of Pure Heart Ministries in St. Louis (pureheartministries.org). The ministry was part of the now-defunct Exodus International, which worked for decades to help free people of "unwanted same-gender attraction" but later shut down and apologized for its actions. (Oddly, the Pure Heart website says its ministry serves the St. Louis "bi-state" region. Just saying.)

"The chances of homosexuality go up . . . if there's a vacuum," Venice said. "Not having a connection with the father is the No. 1 contributing factor in gender identity disorders."

Meanwhile, in "A Parent's Guide to Preventing Homosexuality," clinical psychologist Joseph Nicolosi (josephnicolosi.com) lays out a father's duties:

"He can play rough-and-tumble games with his son . . . help his son learn to throw and catch a ball. He can teach him to pound a wooden peg into a hole in a pegboard, or he can take his son with him into the shower, where the boy cannot help noticing that Dad has a male body, just like he has.

"Psychologists call this process 'incorporating masculinity into a sense of self,' and it is an essential part of growing up straight."

Did we mention that other people don't buy it?

"Gay people realize they are different at all stages in life," said Jean-Marie Navetta, national spokeswoman for Parents, Families and Friends of Lesbians and Gays (PFLAG). "And there aren't 'signs' of it. There are plenty of gruff gay men, and many sensitive straight men who cry more than I do."

She called it "crazy" to try to steer a child a certain way.

"That's been rejected by every major medical and psychological association as not only wrong, but incredibly dangerous. It can lead to depression, self-hatred and even suicide."

The parents here need not fret, but if so inclined can monitor the situation, talk with a group like PFLAG for advice and watch how their son is treated at school.

"If he's gay, they should face their own guilt or second-guessing, almost like a grieving-and-acceptance process," she said. "Then they should be there for their child, gay or not."

Listen up: being deaf doesn't bring on the gay-ness

They asked:

Why are so many deaf men gay? Is it something genetic connected with the disability? Or does it come from early experiences at boarding schools for the deaf?

Scott, 46, straight, Denver

You said:

Being a Deafie myself, I know a lot of deaf gays and lesbians. I've asked them how they "became" gay, and some said it was because of their experiences in the dorm at the schools. It's easy to experiment in those places — raging hormones, kids of the same sex stuffed six to eight in a room ... come on! I went to The Florida School for the Deaf and the Blind, and I can tell you, there are a lot of "out" gays, lesbians, bisexuals there, and a high percentage live in the dorms.

Ashley, deaf straight, St. Augustine

There does seem to be a large number of deaf or hearing-challenged gay men. Guess I need to learn sign language.

B.T., 35, gay male, Philadelphia

Straight deaf people associate mostly with other deaf people, while gay deaf men go to gay bars that are predominantly hearing because there are fewer gay deaf people and they need to date hearing men sometimes. So if you go to a straight bar, you will seldom run into a deaf person, but if you go to a gay bar, you will often see deaf men.

Johnny, 25, gay, Washington

We found:

Nope, there's nothing in the water at schools for the deaf that might cause students to suddenly obsess over ab crunches or redesign each other's rooms. Nor is there an international gay cabal infiltrating the ranks of the deaf.

Still, given the chance to ask a top-notch specialist a really odd question, we'll take it.

No one knows exactly how many gay deaf men there are in the United States, says Virginia Gutman, a clinical psychologist at Gallaudet University, which caters to deaf students. And there aren't scientific studies supporting a genetic link between deafness and homosexuality.

However, "because of using sign language, deaf individuals are very visible at public events," notes Gutman, who authored a chapter on gay-deaf therapy in "Psychotherapy with Deaf Clients from Diverse Groups" (Gallaudet Press). "Hearing people see a group signing [at a gay event] and say, 'Hey, look at all the deaf gay people.' ... Some may not be gay, but instead are heterosexual friends or allies. The impression that is formed may not reflect the reality."

Also, with studies showing less homophobia in the deaf community, deaf gay people are likely more open about their sexual orientation. So it may be easier for them to come out in the general population, further skewing perceptions, she said.

Philip Rubin, former president of the Rainbow Alliance of the Deaf, a national deaf-gay organization, agreed. Oppression against deaf people means a deaf gay person has weathered bias much of his or her life, anyway, so "perhaps we've learned to develop thick skin about being ourselves, whether we're deaf or gay. My motto is 'Life is too short for games.'"

Does campy behavior cramp other gays' style?

They asked:

I was playing sports against this gay guy who was extremely, flamboyantly campy. I was quite turned off. How do you homosexual guys feel about this kind of off-the-chart display?

Joe W., straight, Vancouver, British Columbia

You said:

People who go out of their way to be over the top bother me. This kind of behavior might be fine among friends but is out of place at a sporting event, just as a belching, drunk, beer-bellied football fan would be at a church service.

Jay, 31, gay, Huntsville, Ala.

I know an "in-your-face" gay man. He wants to offend people because he views their reaction as some sort of asinine "litmus test" — if they don't say anything, they're "closeted gay-bashing hypocrites," and if they do, they're "homophobic gay-bashing rednecks." You can't win for losing with this jerk.

Ann, 38, straight, Kansas City, Mo.

I applaud the flamers because they never saw the need to hide who they are. It gave me the courage to come out.

Jeremy, 31, gay, Huntington, W.Va.

It takes all kinds to make up this old world.

Dwanny, 51, lesbian, Fort Worth, Texas

I don't mind fem when it's coming from a friend because it's funny, but when I really sit down and think about it, these are the types of guys available to date — and they don't want to be like guys! I like men for a reason: because they are men!

George, 24, gay, San Antonio

28

We found:

We'd talked about gay issues with University of Massachusetts Amherst Prof. Warren J. Blumenfeld (www.warrenblumenfeld.com) for our book "I Can't Believe You Asked That!" (Perigee). He is the author of "Homophobia: How We All Pay the Price" (Beacon Press) and a top expert on gay culture.

A little explanation of gays and minstrelization here, a sprinkle of camp history there, and we figured we'd be good to go.

Except basically he's had it. Apparently the guy routinely got the Shinola kicked out of him on the playground for acting somewhat gentle, and he's tired of fielding these types of questions.

"Why don't we ever hear the other side? Why don't people call out Schwarzenegger or Bush for being hyper-masculine? Because that's considered a positive attribute," he said. "Anything considered effeminate is hated. Anyone who steps out of their gender role — assertive women, sensitive men — is despised for it."

OK. But isn't it true that even a large chunk of gay men don't like it when other gay men act overly feminine?

"Gay men and lesbians were also raised in our sexist, homophobic culture, which makes us conform to our gender roles. There's a lot of transphobia in the gay community. It is oppression against those who transcend their assigned gender role."

Ultimately, Blumenfeld is proud of gay men who act just as flamboyantly as they please.

"My hat is off to them. They're on the cutting edge of freeing us all from gender roles. Most are targeted for attack. I wish I had the courage to be more expressive than I sometimes am."

I now pronounce you husband and husband?

They asked:

In a heterosexual marriage, there is a "husband" and a "wife." Do married (or similarly committed) homosexual partners think of themselves this way? If so, how do they decide who's who?

Bill, 48, straight, Jacksonville

You said:

It has been my experience in meeting gay couples that one may feel more interest in "womanly" things such as cooking and cleaning, and the other in "manly" things like taking care of the yard and finances.

Gina, 34, straight, North Liberty, Ind.

Just because one mows the lawn, he or she is not "the man." It's typically heterosexuals who feel the need to label one the "husband" and one the "wife."

Michael, 19, gay, Norfolk, Va.

For my partner and me it's a matter of who's willing to assume responsibility for a task. I'm more feminine — the house decorator, more into child rearing — but I'm also more physically aggressive. We don't fit into either mold very well.

Julie, 33, gay, Niles, Ill.

According to modern Christian ideals, a husband will take out the garbage and bring home the beef. A wife will raise the children and keep the house. This antique definition describes few married people I know, of any sexual orientation.

Aysha, 27, female, Ammon, Idaho

Some want a partner who is more "feminine." Others want one more "masculine" — just as some heterosexual men prefer very feminine women while others prefer strong, independent ones.

Tore, 26, gay male, Næstved, Denmark

30

We found:

Looking closer at same-sex relationships can give anyone — straight or gay — a chance to see how people often go on automatic pilot when assuming roles in their relationships, says Janis S. Bohan, a retired psychology professor who's studied sexual orientation and gender roles for more than two decades.

"Maybe we all could learn something by rethinking how we sort roles so that rather than basing them on preconceived notions, we can be more reflective," said Bohan, coauthor of "Conversations About Psychology and Sexual Orientation" (New York University Press).

Many, but not all, same-sex partners assign tasks — who'll wash the car, who'll cook —according to their skills, interests and time constraints rather than society's gender expectations, she noted.

"Straight or gay, we all grew up with heterosexual parents, so for many people these tasks seem to come in bundles that we default to if we don't think about it."

Few gay men or lesbians use labels such as "wife" or "husband," mainly because there's less pressure to do so, she said.

"With my partner, our tasks have changed as our lives have changed. Now that I'm retired, I do more household tasks. But she still sends out the cards and makes the birthday calls. She's always been more in tune to those things than me."

The O.U.T.L.O.U.D.
Method to Dialogue

OPEN UP: This is mostly about opening up to yourself. Why do you want to engage someone? Is it for the right reasons? The answers might help you figure out how to approach another person. A friend once told me the real reason I started Y? wasn't for me to learn more about "Buddhists in Asia or lesbians in San Francisco," but because I wanted to learn something more about myself. He was right. Acknowledging that has helped give me perspective when considering others' answers.

USE YOUR HEAD: Plan for the right question. Not all questions need to be the "wet dogs" variety. Stereotypes and clichés don't work as well as sincere attempts to talk.

TIME IT RIGHT: Create the "O.U.T.L.O.U.D. Moment". Pick your spots for provocative dialogue. Find a genuine opening rather than create a false one. It's often during those down times between all the "vital" discourse that we can most easily find a direct path to someone's point of view. If you spend enough time sitting in the cubicle next to someone of a different culture, chances are there'll come a time — over food, perhaps, or during a power outage — when the topic you've been dying to broach will wend its way naturally into the discussion.

LOCK IN ON THE TARGET: Keeping things simple can give the best chance for getting another's trust and a meaningful reply. Some of the best questions at Y?, those that prompt the most telling answers, are also often the easiest to digest. Remember, it's not about winning your point. It's what comes from the heart that counts most — and captures people's interest. Talking from the heart also means easing into things by letting someone know *why* it would help you to learn the answer to your question before you ask it.

OWN UP TO ASSUMPTIONS: One of the most refreshing and repetitive surprises of the Y? project is the difficulty in predicting how a person will respond to a question. Blacks do not think in lockstep. Nor do whites. Nor Christians or Muslims. Nor gays or straights. Be receptive to another's ideas. Wipe the slate clean and listen to the content of the message, not the color or culture of the messenger.

UNLOAD YOUR EXPECTATIONS: Many of us are thinner-skinned than we'll admit. When we get hit with an answer or comment we hadn't anticipated, our emotions can often get caught off-balance, and our egos get bruised. The solution: Expect the unexpected. You'll never be blindsided or taken aback by information that doesn't gibe with your worldview.

DIGEST THE DIALOGUE: Learning about others doesn't stop when the talking's over. Assess what you're told and how it fits with or departs from your perspectives. Recap your discussion with a third party to distill the most relevant information into its most meaningful points.

ABOUT THE AUTHOR

Phillip J. Milano is the founder of Y? The National Forum on People's Differences, the acclaimed cross-cultural dialogue project that encourages people to ask unflinching, politically incorrect questions about our differences.

Since its creation in 1998, Phillip's web site, YForum.com, has attracted millions of visitors and thousands of questions and answers. He has been featured on CBS, CNN, BET and the BBC, and in numerous newspapers, including The Washington Post, New York Times and USA Today.

He is the author of the Perigee book "I Can't Believe You Asked That!" as well as writer of the pioneering newspaper column/blog "Dare to Ask."

Mr. Milano is a 25-year newspaper veteran. He received his Master of Business Administration from Northern Illinois University and his Bachelor of Science in Journalism from Southern Illinois University.

SPEECHES AND APPEARANCES

Mr. Milano is an in-demand speaker. For bookings, contact

Contemporary Issues Agency
809 Turnberry Drive, Waunakee, WI 53597-2256
Phone: 800-843-2179
Fax: 608-849-6311
www.CIAspeakers.com
Info@CIAspeakers.com

www.ingramcontent.com/pod-product-compliance
Lightning Source LLC
Chambersburg PA
CBHW07045429O526
45791CB00005B/2127